MW00694703

WARNING:

DON'T TRY THIS AT HOME

CONSIDER YOURSELF WARNED!

WARNING:

DON'T TRY THIS AT HOME

By **Ed Wenck** and **Lou Harry**

CIDER MILL PRESS

BOOK PUBLISHERS

Cider Mill Press
Kennebunkport, Maine

Warning: Don't Try This at Home

13-Digit ISBN: 978-1-60433-053-3
10-Digit ISBN: 1-60433-053-8

This book may be ordered by mail from the publisher. Please include $2.50 for postage and handling. Please support your local bookseller first!

Books published by Cider Mill Press Book Publishers are available at special discounts for bulk purchases in the United States by corporations, institutions, and other organizations. For more information, please contact the publisher.

Cider Mill Press Book Publishers
"Where good books are ready for press"
12 Port Farm Road
Kennebunkport, Maine 04046

Visit us on the Web!
www.cidermillpress.com

Design and illustrations by Michael Rogalski
Typography: Impact, Officina Sans, Univers
Printed in China

1 2 3 4 5 6 7 8 9 0
First Edition

Dedication

For
every kid who
ever got grounded—
and then used the downtime
to figure out how to get away
with it on the next
attempt.

—*E.W.*

For everyone
who ever lived
on Wildwood Avenue
in Wildwood, New Jersey.

—*L.H.*

Table of Contents

It's probably best to admit right off the bat that I was a good kid. Good grades. Please and thank you. No arrests, let alone convictions. When teachers left the classroom, I was the one put in charge. When my friends' parents would go out of town, I was the one they told where to find the emergency phone numbers. I was captain of the safety patrol.

I didn't realize what a problem all this would be until I had a son of my own. With a little guy running around the house, I suddenly realized how ill-equipped I was to teach him the ways of the world.

Oh, sure, I could help him learn to tell time, tie his shoes, and figure out how to make change. But when it comes to making a slingshot, hot-wiring a car or, yes, lighting a fart, what useful instruction could I supply?

Knowing that I needed an education—and quick—I went to the one friend who I knew had a history of semi-delinquency and lived to tell about it. I went to Ed.

"Ed," I said, "Help me."

Problem was, there were legal concerns.

"If I go on record telling you this stuff," he said, "and if we put it in a book, won't we be sued if someone does any of this and gets hurt?"

My first thought was that the Ed of thirty years ago would never have said such a thing. Yes, the times have changed. And so we would have to be cautious. Which is why I'm saying for the record:

Don't do any of these things.

In fact, the instructions for each will feature the word "Don't," prominently, at every step. So nobody should make the mistake of thinking that Ed and I actually recommend or endorse doing any of these things.

Don't try this at home. That's part of the title of this book.
So don't.
OK?

Ed's Intro

It's probably best to admit right off the bat that I was a rotten kid. Hellion. Brat. JD. Problem child.

See, it's not that Ma and Pa didn't raise me right. They did. But there were more powerful forces at work. See, I discovered later that my granddad was a low-level gangster, a runner of numbers and liquor for a mob in a major American city back around the time when booze wasn't quite legal. My fondness for mayhem was buried deep within my genes. I let it out as a youngster. As a youngster, I'd be the kid throwing rocks at a kid like Lou. I ran with the crowd that the safety patrol paid for protection.

Between the ages of 8 and 18, I probably only actually did about half the things described herein. The guys I hung out with handled the other half. So I made a few phone calls. Got a little reminder here and there regarding technique. Some of the fellas had long memories and helped me out quite a bit. A few were not accepting phone calls at their current address. You get the picture.

Do I regret some of this stuff? Sure. So why did I agree to do this?

As people get older and have kids, their value systems become similar. Now, Lou's code of conduct and mine aren't very far apart. When we were 13, they were canyons apart. Lou needed help. So, being a friend, and being a reformed hellion, brat, JD and/or problem child, I was the guy.

But there's another reason. Lou wants to let his kid know how dangerous this stuff is. I want a neat, organized place where a dad like me can check for warning signs—see, my boy's a teenager. Yep. I hatched me a younger, quicker, stronger version of myself. Which is why a dad like Lou won't let his daughters out after dark.

So here it is. Some of this stuff seems like harmless fun. Some of it seems absolutely insane. None of it is half as bad as what's in the next book Lou and I are working on:
Don't Try This at Work.

About the Categories

The projects that follow are divided into four categories:

Good, Clean Annoyance
(LOW RISK)

You're Only Hurting Yourself
(PERSONAL PHYSICAL RISK)

A Danger to Others
(RISK OF INJURY TO YOUR FELLOW HUMAN BEINGS)

Possible Jail Time
(LIKE WE SAID, POSSIBLE JAIL TIME)

Now, you don't need a criminal record and/or body cast to know that many of the activities in this book could be placed in any of these categories. But that would be redundant, wouldn't it? What we chose to do is to push each one as far back into the book as possible. That is, if something is likely to risk injury to others and lead to jail time, we put it in the jail time category.

And remember, anything and everything in this book is likely to lead to jail time if a police officer is involved.

We've got nothing but respect and admiration for police officers. Got it?

Good.

DON'T
TRY THIS
AT HOME

1

Good, Clean Annoyance

(LOW RISK)

RISKOMETER

Short-Sheet a Bed

This is a classic summer camp favorite, especially among early teens of the fairer sex. It is totally diabolical when pulled on a older victim—like a randy college roommate who's brought someone home for a little "study break."

DON'T TRY THIS AT HOME...

STEP 1: **DO NOT** remove the flat sheet from a bed.

STEP 2: **DO NOT** replace the flat sheet, only this time tucking the sheet in at the head of the bed the way you'd tuck it in at the foot. Make sure the hospital corners aren't hanging out—fold 'em in and under the mattress.

STEP 3: **DO NOT** spread the flat sheet down toward the foot of the bed, then bring it back up by folding it in half across the bed so the part your victim climbs into looks just like a regularly-made bed.

STEP 4: **DO NOT** wait for your roomie or sorority sister to jam her legs into the little pita sandwich you've just made out of linen while you howl with laughter.

16

STEP 1

STEP 4

Good, Clean Annoyance

17

TP a House

Any chowderhead with enough arm strength can lob a roll of toilet paper over the top of a house or through the branches of a bare tree. It takes a true artist, however, to create the kind of mayhem that'll wind up on YouTube and completely avoid detection in the process. Until your victim sees you on YouTube.

DON'T TRY THIS AT HOME...

STEP 1: **DO NOT** consider the following: Will the owner of my target be at home? If so, will they be sound asleep? What kind of police presence pokes around this neighborhood? Are there any late-night pedestrians about? Any dogs that bark? Any dogs that bite? Any pedestrians that bite? Do I have the moxie and the biceps to get the rolls going over the roof? Over the trees? Should I have picked a ranch house with new landscaping? Is there a fence anywhere on the property? Will it prevent me from sending the roll over the roof in both directions? Will I have time to nail the bushes? Will the homeowner have time to nail me?

STEP 2: **DO NOT** wait for the proper conditions: a damp, dark night with perchance a bit of drizzle in the near-term forecast to really make a muckery of the paper that you're planning to hang.

STEP 3: **DO NOT** purchase **PLENTY** of toilet paper. The formula is: one roll per six linear foot of roofline **OR** six feet of tree height. This is not a time to pick out TP based on thickness, comfort, absorbency, or squeezeability. You would want the longest possible rolls for the lowest possible cost if you were to do this. Which you won't.

STEP 4: **DO NOT** wear dark clothing and park a block away, creeping catlike toward the target and carrying your ammo in a large backpack. **DO NOT** wear running shoes.

STEP 4

STEP 5: **DO NOT** peel a foot or so of TP off the roll so that it unspools in flight. **DO NOT** grab this 'tail' in your non-throwing hand. **DO NOT** lob the roll over the roof. **DO NOT** run around the back of the house, grab what's left of the roll, and repeat. And repeat And repeat. And so on. And so on … (**NOTE:** Two or more vandals can play a kind of catch with the rolls back and forth on either side of the house, cutting their TP time by as much as two-thirds.) **CAUTION:** A fat roll of Quilted Northern thunking on asphalt shingles may wake the homeowner. (Remember the running shoes?)

STEP 5

WARNING: Don't Try This at Home

STEP 6: **DO NOT** repeat this process on every tree in the yard. **DO NOT** roll TP across hedges or bushes. **DO NOT** jam wads of TP among branches in the shrubbery. **DO NOT** wrap fences, lampposts, mailboxes, and lawn jockeys.

STEP 7: **DO NOT** drive past your target the next day, howling with laughter as Cranky Neighbor bellows heavenward, cursing the constable, the local educational institutions, and the neighborhood watch association.

Good, Clean Annoyance

Steam Open a Letter

You're suspicious, eh? Suspicious enough to steam open a letter to find out what somebody else is up to—without their knowledge of the act? Suspicious enough to break a long-established bond of trust on your part—and maybe feel miserable because you've been proven wrong—or even worse, feel miserable because you were proven right? Suspicious enough to commit the federal offense of mail tampering?
Great!

DON'T TRY THIS AT HOME...

STEP 1: **DO NOT** boil about two inches of water in a medium saucepan.

STEP 2: **DO NOT** hold an envelope flap side down, just above where the steam is hot enough to really burn your fingers.

STEP 3: **DO NOT** find a loose spot where you can insert a finger under the flap.

STEP 4: **DO NOT** work your fingers slowly across the flap as the glue melts. This is tricky. Go too slow, and the paper will get soggy and wrinkly; go too fast, and it'll rip. Either way, the jig is up.

WARNING: Don't Try This at Home

STEP 5: DO NOT read the enclosed tax return or love letter or collection notice while the envelope dries.

STEP 6: DO NOT reinsert the contents of the envelope, then moisten and reseal the flap.

STEP 7: DO NOT confront the mail's intended recipient about his or her empty bank account, fraudulent deductions, or cheatin' heart.

Sure, you can debate the relative value of the second set of properties on each side of the board, you can crunch numbers that'll tell you the orange spaces are the ones to own because of their proximity to jail, you can argue right through the weekend about whether or not buying a utility is any damn good at all—or you can be the banker and steal.

See? This game really is like modern economics! The big trick here is to build your pile slowly and early. A losing banker who suddenly gets rich toward the end of regulation play will wind up in front of a grand jury.

DON'T TRY THIS AT HOME...

STEP 1: **DO NOT** volunteer to be the banker.

STEP 2: **DO NOT** acquire as many large bills in your personal stash as possible.

STEP 3: **DO NOT,** when asked to make change for another player, go ahead and make change for yourself during the same transaction.

STEP 4: **DO NOT** take a little interest during both transactions. Example: If a player with a 100-dollar bill asks you for tens, **DO NOT** count 11 and slip the last ten under the hundred.

24

STEP 1

STEP 5: **DO NOT** pull another hundred off your pile and repeat the process, deftly transferring the two extra tens to your stack.

Better sleight-of-hand artists can drop the extra cash into their pile without making change for themselves. Use a mirror to practice. Go ahead. There's nothing to feel ashamed about. It's only play money, right? Right?

Of course, there are other ways **NOT** to do it:

STEP 1: DO NOT roll and immediately realize that your five will put you on Boardwalk, where rent is now akin to a condo at Trump Plaza.

STEP 2: DO NOT quickly over- or under-count your move so you dodge that space by shuffling the little race car four or six spaces. An under-count works best because it's easy to double-clutch one space. (Getting caught is less likely if the new space involves paying a landlord and does not involve hitting "Go.") This always works with slightly drunk adults. It never works with really drunk

STEP 2

WARNING: Don't Try This at Home

adults or kids. The latter two groups will always call you on it. Especially the kids. And they fight dirty.

And there's the old standby:

STEP 1: **DO NOT**, when no one is looking, move your piece to a more advantageous space.

Fake a UFO Photo

Unlike the other dubious activities warned AGAINST in this handy volume, faking a UFO photo actually puts you in the company of generations of people who have tried to legitimize their wacky stories and garner media attention.

But don't get us started on that. Instead, just take your fancy-schmancy Photoshop programs and your computer-generated clip art of little green men and spaceships and Yoda and stuff 'em. Old-school film in a Kodak camera will always, for our money, yield the best results.

OK, use your digital camera if you have to, but plan on burning through a dozen shots until you get the winner.

DON'T TRY THIS AT HOME...

STEP 1: **DO NOT** cut about an inch from the length of an empty toilet-paper tube. (You don't have these kicking around from your adventures not TP-ing a house, right?)

STEP 2: **DO NOT** tape said tube to the middle of the top of a Frisbee©.

STEP 3: **DO NOT** throw this thing repeatedly up in the air toward the sun, shooting photo after photo until you get an image of a blurry, unearthly object that seems to zip by

WARNING: Don't Try This at Home

STEP 3

and/or over houses, cars, and trees and looks absolutely nothing like a Wham-O disc with some cardboard on top.

While we're at it, the other great bit of folklore fakery requires a costume and a live setting. We're talking about how to ...

Fake a Bigfoot Sighting

STEP 1: **DO NOT** rent a gorilla suit.

STEP 2: **DO NOT** lie in wait along a wooded country road at night.

STEP 3: **DO NOT** lift up menacingly out of the thicket at the first sign of headlights, raise your arms, scream, and disappear into the bush.

STEP 4: **DO NOT** have a friend take photographs in low light of this same scene, using the headlights of his car, and then send them to a local newspaper for publication.

The good news is that, since you didn't do any of this, you don't have to pray the guys in the car don't have guns!

STEP 3

WARNING: Don't Try This at Home

Make a Prank Call

Let's be clear: You shouldn't prank people on the phone and tape the poor slob on the other end to preserve your stupidity for the ages. It's illegal in most states. It's also annoying and obnoxious for the prankee.

Of course, for the prankster and his buds, it's pretty darn hilarious.

DON'T TRY THIS AT HOME...

STEP 1: DO NOT go to Radio Shack and pick up a phone interface that will plug a land line into a computer with recording software. (The guys at Radio Shack can walk anyone through this with the latest gear. They live for this stuff. Well, that and getting your zip code.)

STEP 2: DO NOT call a motel in Nevada, where it's legal for one party to tape a phone call without the other party's knowledge.

STEP 3: DO NOT, when the clerk answers, say: "Hi, this is John Razzmeth from True Blue Port-A-Potty. We're about to pull off the interstate, and we just wanted to confirm the drop-off location on where you'd like these port-a-potties delivered."

STEP 1

STEP 4: **DO NOT** wait for the clerk to say, "I don't know anything about a delivery of port-a-potties."

STEP 5: **DO NOT** respond: "I have it right here on the delivery paperwork ... " [*shuffle papers and pretend you're asking your driver to pull over just up ahead, as there may be a problem ... then continue*] "... Let me confirm—this is the [*insert name of motel here*] at [*insert the street address, which you've looked up before making the call*], correct? OK, we'll be there in a few minutes, but do you have a parking lot in the back? We try to be as discreet as we can when a motel is having plumbing issues."

WARNING: Don't Try This at Home

STEP 6: DO NOT wait for the clerk to say, "But I don't know anything about plumbing issues. I think our plumbing is working fine."

STEP 7: DO NOT say, "Well, we have 15 bright-blue port-a-potties loaded onto our vehicles that say otherwise." [*insert chuckle here*] "Why don't you meet us out front in a few minutes? That way you can sign for these, and we can be on our way. Just listen for our big truck. It will be hard for you to miss us, as there will be a loud sloshing sound when we hit the brakes. See ya in 10 minutes. Bye-Bye!"

STEP 5

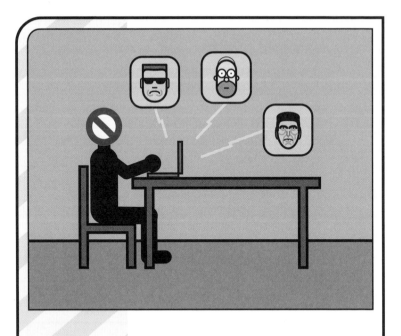

Alternate strategy:

DO NOT surf the Internet for celebrity soundboards, which allow a phone prankster to play audio clips of voices such those of Arnold Schwarzenegger, Homer Simpson, or Al Pacino, and use those clips to carry on a conversation with an unsuspecting rube. Most soundboards are broken down into categories such as "Greetings," "Responses," and so forth, almost as if some wise guy had ignored our advice and pranked some poor old lady in Reno.

WARNING: Don't Try This at Home

Make a Mentos® and Soda Pop Geyser

Mentos® breath mints have been known forever by their tagline, "The Freshmaker." In the past few years, another name might have become more accurate: "The Spraymaker." Just add some soda.

The popularity of this little stunt is a real testament to the power of YouTube. A science reporter named Steve Spangler on a TV news show in Denver first showed the locals how to pull this off in the fall of 2005, and the online video picked up enough hits to propel Spangler to an appearance on the Ellen show two years later.

The concept is pretty simple: A roll of Mentos® dropped into a two-liter bottle of pop has enough geyser-producing power to recreate the legendary Brady Bunch backyard-volcano scene. Want to soak Marcia? Press on.

DON'T TRY THIS AT HOME...

STEP 1: **DO NOT** buy a roll of Mentos® and a two-liter bottle of soda. Diet is less sticky than regular, and seems to foam a bit more, but if you want a replica of Old Faithful that's gonna draw every yellow jacket in five states to your back porch, use the sugared stuff.

STEP 2: **DO NOT** open the soda. **DO NOT** roll the Mentos® into a paper tube that'll hold them loosely.

STEP 3: **DO NOT**, while holding your cylinder of Freshmakers in the palm of your hand with the open end of the tube pointing skyward, place a playing card flat over the open end.

STEP 4: **DO NOT** flip the card-and-tube assembly over the nozzle of the bottle so that the card is acting as a barrier between the tube of candy and the pop. **DO NOT** position your Mentos® so they'll all drop in at once when you pull the card free.

STEP 5: **DO NOT** pull the card free.

STEP 6: **DO NOT** run. Hopefully, the camera taping this for the Internet video is waterproof.

STEP 6

WARNING: Don't Try This at Home

So you've decided that your 1989 Buick LeSabre is only good for two things: world's biggest paperweight, or demolition derby entrant. A little Web surfing will tell you where to find the closest redneck dirt-track smash-'em-up event. The winners of these things usually pick up anywhere from a few hundred to a few thousand bucks, depending on the number of cars paying an entry fee.

Every one of these contests has a specific set of rules: what you can weld to your car, where to locate your gas tank, how often you need to drive into somebody else, whether or not you need a mental evaluation to get into the ring, and so on.

Once you've got your ride rigged and painted and de-glassified, you'll need to spend three or four days practicing driving in reverse. Why? Press on.

(All this, of course, assumes that the demolition derby in question is a legitimate one, not just some bored friends in an empty lot.)

DON'T TRY THIS AT HOME...

STEP 1: **DO NOT** find the bulkiest car imaginable.

STEP 2: **DO NOT** follow all the derby's rules regarding contact and vehicle modifications *TO THE LETTER*.

STEP 3: **DO NOT** keep moving once the green flag flies.

STEP 4: **DO NOT** avoid the corners. Walls are not your friend.

STEP 5: **DO NOT** strike other drivers **SQUARELY** in the **FRONT** of their vehicle with the **REAR** of your vehicle. The idea is to take out the other guy's motor and/or radiator first. Your engine ain't in the trunk, right? Not that it matters where your engine is, because you're not going to do any of this, are you?

STEP 6: **DO NOT** dodge other drivers by backing away at an angle so they can't hit you squarely.

STEP 5

WARNING: Don't Try This at Home

STEP 8

STEP 7: **DO NOT** have the last running ride to make contact.

STEP 8: **DO NOT** receive a fat check, a cheap trophy, and a smooch from the track's Skoal-in-her-teeth hillbilly hottie.

This chapter was originally about how to actually cover your tracks. Like in Last of the Mohicans or something. But they'll teach you that kind of thing in the Boy Scout Handbook. You might even get a badge for it. Instead, it makes more sense in this book to discuss covering a different kind of tracks.

DON'T TRY THIS AT HOME...

STEP 1: **DO NOT** attend a gentlemen's club in the daytime when you'd normally be at work. OK, maybe the talent isn't the best, but come on— you're doing this on the sly. Or rather, not doing it on the sly.

STEP 2: **DO NOT** pay in cash. Do we really have to explain this?

STEP 3: **DO NOT** buy your wife perfume on the way home. A savvy customer of the average adult-entertainment facility knows that the nose can detect the biggest track of all: the unmistakable baby-powder smell left behind by your garden-variety exotic dancer. If you tell the wife you've been thinking about her all day and wanted to pick up something for her that would smell really, really good; well, a few samples on **YOUR** wrists will mask the scent of stripper from your old lady's sniffer.

WARNING: Don't Try This at Home

Good, Clean Annoyance

41

If we learned anything at all from the Discovery Channel, it's that folks in other countries use Creepy Crawler critters as a part of their regular diet. This is one of many reasons why your humble authors remain American.

Yet we all stood in awe of The Kid Who Would Eat Anything for Money when, in fourth grade, he devoured a cricket. Then, in sixth grade, when he lunched on a worm. And then, of course, in 10th grade, when it was the worm at the bottom of a bottle of mescal.

Of course, the non-wormy contents of the bottle of mescal sent him to the hospital to have his stomach pumped. Remember?

If you find yourself needing to equal this kid—or be this kid—the best way to go is with either grasshoppers or crickets. Flies enjoy things that you wouldn't enjoy, and spiders might be poisonous. Anything with a stinger is clearly out.

DON'T TRY THIS AT HOME...

STEP 1: **DO NOT** catch a grasshopper.

STEP 2: **DO NOT** put him in a mason jar and fill it up with water. This drowns the bug and washes him at the same time.

STEP 3: **DO NOT** wash the insect one more time.

WARNING: Don't Try This at Home

STEP 4

(**NOTE:** At this point, you could safely consume the animal. But why not cover the gourmet route, since you're not going to do this anyway?)

STEP 4: **DO NOT** heat some lovely extra-virgin olive oil in a skillet.

STEP 5: **DO NOT** cook the critter until he's crispy.

STEP 6: **DO NOT** drain and cool the bug on paper towels.

STEP 7: **DO NOT** season with salt or pepper or soy sauce or hot sauce or *herbes de Provence*.

STEP 8: **DO NOT** chow down.

The good news is that since you haven't done any of this, you don't have to worry about your name being on a PETA watch-list.

WARNING: Don't Try This at Home

Make an Elderly Driver Panic at a Red Light

Ed actually pulled this off to great effect with a buddy many years ago in Ocean City, Maryland. The conditions were perfect: busy intersection, three lanes on either side of a flat two-way street, nobody behind any of the cars involved, twilight, and a hat-headed geezer at the wheel of a Caddy in the center lane.

DON'T TRY THIS AT HOME...

STEP 1: **DO NOT** wait for an elderly driver to pull up to a red light in the center lane of a three-lane road.

STEP 1

Good, Clean Annoyance

STEP 2: **DO NOT**, using an accomplice in a second car, pull up on either side of the crusty ol' fart in the middle.

STEP 3: **DO NOT** shift your car into reverse as your buddy does the same.

STEP 4: **DO NOT**, after ensuring nobody's behind you or your buddy in each respective lane, slowly back up at the same time, giving the old guy in the middle the illusion that he's drifting forward into the intersection.

WARNING: Don't Try This at Home

STEP 5: **DO NOT** howl with laughter as the poor old fellow stomps furiously on his brake pedal, convinced that he's about to be T-boned by traffic flying in from his left and right.

Sure, this will work on occasion without an accomplice, but the technique using two cars on either side of the victim is a guaranteed hit.

So, how in the world does the little Japanese guy usually stomp the big fat goons at the annual Nathan's Hot Dog Eating Contest in NYC?

Training, baby.

Takeru Kobayashi is a prime physical specimen who's learned how to distend his demure stomach to the limits of its volume. The average human food-bag holds about a quart under normal circumstance. By beginning your training two to three months ahead of time, you can stretch your belly till it holds four times that amount.

DON'T TRY THIS AT HOME...

STEP 1: **DO NOT** pick a date at least 60 days prior to your upcoming contest.

STEP 2: **DO NOT** see a doctor and tell him what you're doing. (Hopefully he can give advice on how to pull it off properly given one's own unique physical state.)

STEP 3: **DO NOT** gradually stretch your stomach by eating as much lettuce or watermelon as you comfortably can in one sitting.

STEP 4: **DO NOT** slowly increase that amount of lettuce or watermelon by adding a little more volume every day.

WARNING: Don't Try This at Home

STEP 5: DO NOT stay in shape. A band of fat around the middle may actually **IMPEDE** the stomach's ability to stretch.

STEP 6: DO NOT practice your hand-eye coordination. TiVo Kobayashi. Learn his moves, Grasshopper.

STEP 7: On the big day, **DO NOT** use water strategically. For example: Kobayashi ingests water by dipping halves of the hot dog buns in a glass of water and eating them separately from the franks. It makes the buns slide more easily and keeps his gullet greased for the franks.

STEP 8: **DO NOT** wiggle your midsection while you eat. This actually settles the chow more compactly in the stomach.

If you don't do this, you won't suddenly realize you've eaten 12,000 calories on ESPN2 while CNN is showing endless footage of starving African kids at exactly the same time. Nice going, creep.

WARNING: Don't Try This at Home

There are those who walk among us who may truthfully utter the phrase "I never win anything." Then there are those who seem to be fed, sheltered, clothed and concert-ticketed by every radio station in town.

The trick?

There ain't none.

Besides persistence. And a land line. Or twenty.

The one thing that we can tell you that will never, ever work is a sob story. The DJ you're cryin' to knows you're Kenny Chesney's Number One Fan. The rules state he's gotta give away the tickets in a way that attempts to give everybody a shot. Additionally, the next time you're at one of Kenny Chesney's concerts, look around. The other 39,999 people with you are all his Number One Fans, too.

DON'T TRY THIS AT HOME...

STEP 1: **DO NOT** land a job working a switchboard, phone bank, or call-center that has multiple outgoing land lines, all with a speed-dial function. The perfect gig would also provide other employees/contestants who are in cahoots with you.

STEP 2: **DO NOT** play close attention to a radio station's contest promos and/or announcements. Stations have gotten very generous about telling you exactly when to listen and win.

Good, Clean Annoyance

STEP 3: **DO NOT**, at the very moment you're instructed to call, have everybody in the joint dial the station's request number on every available land line. (Here's why it's important to have land lines: Cellular callers are often met with the old "All circuits are busy" *Close Encounters of the Third Kind* musical tones, since they're on a grid that's a heck of a lot more popular than your daddy's old fashioned hardwired network.)

STEP 4: **DO NOT** have a winner quit the next time the cue to call is played. If that winner repeats as caller 1,000,097, he won't get another prize. The person at 1,000,098 will.

WARNING: Don't Try This at Home

STEP 5

STEP 5: **DO NOT** wait 30 days and try again. And again. And again. See? You've gotten so good at this that your favorite radio personality has given you a new nickname: "Prize Pig."

Steal a Wireless Internet Connection

The premise here is pretty simple: a bunch of folks in your neighborhood have probably installed wireless routers. A wireless router is an Internet connection that needs nary a cable to bring the World Wide Web to your little old Dell.

At least one of those knuckleheads hasn't gone through the steps necessary to encrypt the signal. That means that anybody in range, on any computer at all that's capable of pulling in a wireless Internet feed, can look at naughty pictures using his neighbor's Web connection.

DON'T TRY THIS AT HOME...

STEP 1: **DO NOT** take a laptop with a wireless receiver card and a fully charged battery with you in your car.

STEP 2: **DO NOT** drive around your neighborhood with the "Connect to" menu open, hunting for a signal that's wide open and ready to party.

WARNING: Don't Try This at Home

STEP 1

STEP 2

Good, Clean Annoyance

Fake an Illness

The one thing that actors in the sick-bed theatre know is that most symptoms are unprovable. "I don't feel good" is often met with skepticism from, say, your girlfriend who knows you haven't been preparing for that presentation you're supposed to do today. Your tummy hurts? A little case of the sniffles? Humbug. Really sick people have one thing in common: a fever.

DON'T TRY THIS AT HOME...

STEP 1: **DO NOT** make sure the thermometer is easy to find.

STEP 5

WARNING: Don't Try This at Home

STEP 2: **DO NOT** hold as much hot water in your mouth, as warm as you can stand it.

STEP 3: **DO NOT** lay a cool, damp washcloth over your forehead to make you feel all clammy.

SPEP 4: **DO NOT** lose the washcloth and the hot water when you hear your girlfriend coming upstairs to see why you're not sitting down in front of your steamin' plate of flapjacks.

STEP 5: **DO NOT** complain to her about a fever.

STEP 6: **DO NOT** spend the day at a Cubs game with your loser friend Cameron.

STEP 6

Make Yourself Vomit

We have no idea why anyone would want to vomit voluntarily. Ed, in fact, is in the middle of a near-decade-long streak of vomit-free living.

You, however, have decided you need to either exit a party, stop the spins, or simply make room for more. Godspeed.

DON'T TRY THIS AT HOME...

STEP 1: **DO NOT**, without touching your uvula—you remember what Mom told you about touching your uvula, right?—stick one finger toward the back of your throat until you trigger your gag reflex. A spoon will also work.

STEP 2: **DO NOT** regurgitate, vomit, purge, expel, spew, puke, yak, boot, hurl, ralph, toss your cookies, lose your lunch, max out the Heimlich, blow chunks, retch, heave, drive the porcelain bus, or show 'em the Technicolor yawn.

WARNING: Don't Try This at Home

STEP 1

STEP 2

Good, Clean Annoyance

Give a Hickey

In spring, a young man's fancy lightly turns to thoughts of love. Then follows the overeager make-out session, which may result in a "love bite," "vampire kiss," "white-trash necklace," or "hickey."

Why, you ask? Testosterone.

Why not? 'Cause her old man will definitely know you've been making out with his daughter, dimwit.

DON'T TRY THIS AT HOME...

STEP 1: **DO NOT** begin dating the kind of girl who will let you do this sort of thing. Seriously. Didn't you pay attention to your mother at all? You're gonna catch something.

STEP 3

WARNING: Don't Try This at Home

STEP 2: DO NOT, in the throes of a steamy round of smoochin', work your way down to the side of her neck.

STEP 3: DO NOT, upon finding a sufficiently tender area that makes her gasp a little when you nibble, part your lips and teeth and apply suction until she squeals just a tad. This usually indicates you've probably left a mark, ya big goon.

STEP 4: DO NOT sit sullenly in your Camaro as she tells you through the driver's side window that she can't go out tonight because her dad didn't buy that story about how she burned herself with the curling iron.

DON'T
TRY THIS
AT HOME

2

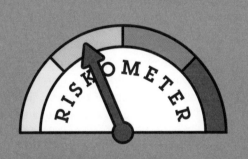

You're Only
Hurting Yourself
(PERSONAL PHYSICAL RISK)

Jump Anything on a Bicycle

OK, if you insist on stuff like this, wear a helmet. We want you to be able to finish this book without having your girlfriend or wife read it to you while she's sitting next to your hospital bed, comprende?

DON'T TRY THIS AT HOME...

STEP 1: DO NOT build a launch ramp. Whether you make it outta dirt or plywood and cinderblocks (bricks will usually collapse during the jump if you stack more than one), you need an angle low enough so that your front wheel won't think that your ramp is really a wall and send your keister over the handlebars.

STEP 2: DO NOT build a finish ramp. Yeah, something that will angle your bike back on to terra firma is a step most kids overlook. Slamming onto a flat surface makes for a bad back later in life.

STEP 3: DO NOT ask your best friend to lie down between the ramps so you can prove you've mastered the skill.

STEP 4: DO NOT pedal as fast as you can ... toward the ramp ... geez, we really can't watch the rest of this.

WARNING: Don't Try This at Home

STEP 1

STEP 4

You're Only Hurting Yourself

Stage a Supermarket-Cart Race

The problem with go-carts is nobody has a go-cart. But everyone has a supermarket within a reasonable distance from home. And every supermarket has extra shopping carts that aren't being used. (Ask yourself: Have you ever seen a supermarket run out of them?) Voilà, you've got yourself a makeshift go-cart.

With a few challenges, of course. For one, a shopping cart will not run on its own steam, so racing them requires a hill and/or two-person teams. (Even with a hill, someone has to get you started.)

Second, a shopping cart has no brakes—which is only a problem if you plan on, at some point, stopping.

Third, a shopping cart is designed to carry food items, not human beings larger than toddlers.

So you've got some challenges.

DON'T TRY THIS AT HOME...

STEP 1: **DO NOT** visit your nearest 24-hour supermarket under cover of darkness.

STEP 2: **DO NOT** identify two (non-motorized) carts with relatively smooth motion for all four wheels. The ones with the big red plastic cars in front are probably not a good idea, either.

WARNING: Don't Try This at Home

STEP 3: **DO NOT** liberate these carts from the supermarket parking lot (a surprisingly difficult task without a pickup truck—yet two shopping carts in a pickup truck are a very suspicious and conspicuous sight).

STEP 4: **DO NOT** take the carts to a hill that doesn't lead into traffic.

STEP 5: **DO NOT** securely fashion the crash helmets that you brought with you because, trust us, the helmets will earn their name.

STEP 6: **DO NOT** have one member from each team climb into the main basket of the cart. If the cart is a swing-back model—in which the side closest to the cart-pusher swings up and into the basket—and if you are short, **DO NOT** consider positioning this over the passenger and using it as a roof.

STEP 7: At the count of three, **DO NOT** give the riders enough of a push to get the carts rolling downhill.

STEP 8: Betting on who gets to the bottom first is absurd. Instead, **DO NOT** bet on who will stay in the cart the longest ... and not end up in the ER.

STEP 7

WARNING: Don't Try This at Home

Put a Car Into a Four-Wheel Drift

Of all the things we've warning you against, this Japanese import is the one that we find the most flat-out bananas. Throwing a car into a turn and letting the entire rig slide before you steer into and then out of your drift—well, you're messing with Mother Nature's righteous inclination to let centrifugal force roll your Honda into somebody's flowerbeds.

If you really enjoy eating your all of your meals through a straw, then by all means, go for it. Let us know how it went when you come out of the coma. Domo Arigato, Mr. Moron-o.

The technique described below is the beginner's model. It's called an "E-drift" by all those crazy kids who've played too many video games and decided to check out what it really feels like to jam one's face through a windshield in the non-virtual world.

DON'T TRY THIS AT HOME...

STEP 1: **DO NOT** place your keister into a rear-wheel-drive car with a manual transmission.

STEP 2: **DO NOT** find a wide a corner and enter at a comfortable speed.

STEP 3: **DO NOT**, with the clutch depressed, pull up on the hand brake.

STEP 4: **DO NOT**, as soon as traction is lost, release the clutch and floor the accelerator.

STEP 5: **DO NOT** counter-steer. (If you don't know what "counter-steer" means, you really should've abandoned this idea just prior to Step 3.)

STEP 6: **DO NOT** regain control as you exit the corner. Go ahead and wind up in your neighbor's yard and/or living room and/or swimming pool.

WARNING: Don't Try This at Home

Drag Race in the Street

This is with bicycles, right? You're not going to actually try this with your girlfriend's Honda, right? Right?

DON'T TRY THIS AT HOME...

STEP 1: **DO NOT** find an empty, unoccupied, traffic-free half-mile stretch of straight, flat road with treeless shoulders and no cops.

STEP 2: **DO NOT** mark off the quarter-mile from the beginning to the middle of that half-mile run, placing a neutral spotter (or two) at the finish line.

STEP 3: **DO NOT** line up your ride side by side with your enemy's, making sure the nose of each vehicle is perfectly in line at the starting point. **YOU'D BETTER NOT HAVE ANYBODY ELSE IN THE CAR.** Passengers can alter the weight distribution of a speeding vehicle pretty dramatically, especially when they're screaming in terror.

STEP 4: **DO NOT** place a purty young thing holding a flashlight between and just ahead of both drivers. She should be facing the cars and pointing the flashlight forward so the drivers can see the lamp.

You're Only Hurting Yourself

STEP 5: **DO NOT** put your ride in neutral, depress the brake to the floor, and rev the engine once. **DON'T** feel the brake pedal sink deeper to the floor. **DON'T** hold the brake down.

STEP 6: **DO NOT** instruct your starter to flick the "on" switch three times in a smooth 1-2-3 count: on-off, on-off, on. The third light means go.

STEP 7: **DO NOT,** as the count begins, slowly rev your engine up, holding the car still with the foot brake.

STEP 8: **DO NOT,** when the light comes on the third time, release the brake and floor the gas simultaneously. Bye-bye! We'll see your wreckage in a drivers' ed film someday!

STEP 8

WARNING: Don't Try This at Home

Turn Kids' Games Into Drinking Games

This is pretty simple: Just add liquor. The notion of corrupting a kid's game with adult libations follows this formula: If it's a small event, drink one or more times. If it's a big event, chug. Be mindful that shots can put you under very quickly. This is why drinking games are usually played with beer.

Any kid's game from Rock Paper Scissors to tic-tac-toe can be adapted, but for the purpose of expansive illustration, here's one with a board game. To avoid copyright infringement, we'll call this particular game "Candytown."

DON'T TRY THIS AT HOME...

STEP 1: **DO NOT** begin play as you normally would save for the addition of a brewski or six at each player's side.

STEP 2: **DO NOT** drink once every time you draw a card telling you to move to the **SECOND** colored block.

STEP 3: **DO NOT** drink **TWICE** if a drawing a character card moves you backward. **DO NOT** drink three times if drawing a character card moves you forward.

STEP 4: **DO NOT** drink once for every turn your game piece is stuck in a sticky spot.

STEP 5: **DO NOT** chug your beer if you land on a shortcut and jump ahead.

STEP 6: **DO NOT** chug your beer if you finish first.

If you enjoyed not doing this, you might also enjoy not violating other games, like such as ... umm, let's call it "Sliding Boards and Stairsteps."

WARNING: Don't Try This at Home

Rappel Off Your Chimney

Here's a great way to convince your neighbors that you were in the armed forces, even if the closest you got to military service was a knot-tying merit badge in your Webelos troop at age 10. We can't think of any other reason for doing this unless you're looking to make a dramatic descent after replacing a few shingles.

We'll start with the notion that you're already on your roof. How you got up there, we don't know. We're just here to get your tail down. Good luck, G.I. Joe.

DON'T TRY THIS AT HOME...

STEP 1: Using water knots, **DO NOT** tie three 10-foot strips of tubular webbing into loops that can be hitched to a sturdy part at the top of your chimney. **DO NOT** ensure that the anchor you're hooking onto won't give way or allow the webbing to slip downward while you're rappelling. (We'll bet a bunch of you just gave up on this one and set the book down to go buy a ladder.) **DO NOT** double- and triple-check this rig.

STEP 2: **DO NOT** attach two locking carabiners to the three loose loop ends as you hold the ends together. **DO NOT** lock both carabiners.

STEP 3: **DO NOT** step into the harness

STEP 4: **DO NOT** attach a climbing rope equal in length to the height of your chimney plus **AT LEAST** twenty feet extra to the carabiners using a double figure eight or bowline knot.

STEP 5: **DO NOT** loop your rope into the large end of a figure eight rappelling device, passing the loop behind the small end of the figure eight.

WARNING: Don't Try This at Home

STEP 6: **DO NOT**, using another locking carabiner, clip the small end of the figure eight to the loop in the front of the tightened rappelling harness that's squeezing the life outta your man-parts.

STEP 7: **DO NOT** put on a pair of heavy leather gloves.

STEP 8: **DO NOT**, if you are right-handed, grip the rope **BELOW** the figure eight device with your right hand at your hip, while the left hand grips the rope above the figure eight at a level roughly near the sternum.

STEP 6

You're Only Hurting Yourself

STEP 9: **DO NOT**, holding your right fist with the knuckles pointing downward toward your feet and gripping the rope tightly, ease your weight into the butt of the harness, working yourself into a nearly sitting position as your feet lay flat against the side of your chimney.

STEP 10: **DO NOT** bring your right hand slightly behind your hip as you begin to walk down the side of the chimney, releasing the rope ever so slightly as you make your way down. The more you release, the faster you'll move. Gripping tightly with your right hand will stop your descent.

STEP 10

WARNING: Don't Try This at Home

STEP 11: **DO NOT** slow your descent gradually before you stop—sudden stops can damage your equipment. Also, moving too quickly can literally melt the rope onto your gloves. This is the part where the fire department comes in—to put you out, then pull you off the side of your house.

STEP 12: **DO NOT**, upon reaching the ground, unlock your carabiner, and then wonder how you're gonna get all that rappelling crap off the top of your chimney.

We're assuming here you've got some experience on a skateboard. We're also assuming you've got the sense to wear a helmet when you're on said skateboard.

On the other hand, if you got enough sense to buy a brain bucket, why'd you buy this book?

The notion of skating in empty pools goes back to the California drought of the late 70s. A rotten economy and a serious lack of rain led to a bumper crop of abandoned, bone-dry, backyard in-ground pools around L.A. Some intrepid skaters who were willing to trespass were followed by some equally intrepid kids with cameras. The films and photos made their way around the states, and pretty soon, if an empty pool was to be found anywhere from Iowa to Texas to Delaware, some knuckle-headed teenager was probably skating in it. Tubular!

DON'T TRY THIS AT HOME...

STEP 1: **DO NOT** find an empty—preferably abandoned, or at least, on the grounds of an unoccupied home—swimming pool with **ROUNDED** corners where the walls meet the bottom. Oval or kidney-shaped pools work best; obviously, smoother junctions and wider radiuses on the corners are optimum. Awesome!

WARNING: Don't Try This at Home

STEP 2

STEP 2: **DO NOT** drop in by pushing yourself off the coping (the concrete lip around the pool) at the top of the **SHALLOW** end. If you did, you would pick up speed as your traversed the bottom of the pool, but you could use your push leg for a little more. Stoked!

STEP 3: **DO NOT** skate toward the deep end, then up the wall, kick-turning (lifting the front wheels off the ground and turning on the rears) at the apex of your vertical trip. Radical!

STEP 4: **DO NOT** repeat this in a serpentine fashion throughout the pool, using all sides of the concrete, steadily gaining enough height so that your back axle is grinding off the coping at the top of your turn. Big Kahuna!

STEP 5: **DO NOT** knock this off when the light starts to dim. A misstep from 7 or 8 feet up pretty much guarantees you'll be eating all your meals through a straw for six weeks. Dumbass!

WARNING: Don't Try This at Home

STEP 5

Since you haven't been doing this, you won't have to figure out how to get out of the empty pool.

This is tricky, dangerous, and ultimately, of course, dishonest. Card cheats go to hell; bad card cheats get there quicker. And more damaged. There's a reason why we put this in the personal injury section. Card players are not generally known as a forgiving lot.

There's a million ways to cheat at cards. This way is designed for a penny-ante game of beginners playing entry-level Five Card Draw with nothing wild. Those who aim to cheat at Texas Hold 'Em should first pick up a book full of tips on how to keep from getting beaten up in prison.

DON'T TRY THIS AT HOME...

STEP 1: **DO NOT** acquire a deck that's exactly like the one you'll be using in tonight's friendly little game.

STEP 2: **DO NOT** lay out the deck ahead of time so that every value is piled together in groups of four (or however many will be at your table).

STEP 3: **DO NOT** begin stacking cards so that every fourth card dealt from the top of the deck is an ace. Your first four cards might read 2, 5, 10, Ace; the second group would be Jack, 3, 10, Ace; and so on. Please note that the third player dealt to is being given a decent hand. If player two has two pair, for example, they'll be more apt to run a pot against the dealer's four of a kind. After the five cards each player would be dealt initially have been arranged and the dealer has all the aces, the rest of the drawn cards don't mean anything. They can be shuffled up and stuck on the bottom of the deck.

STEP 4: **DO NOT** pocket your rigged deck, surreptitiously pulling it out of your pants and onto your lap when the time is right for the big hand.

STEP 5: **DO NOT,** when it's your turn to deal, shuffle up and then pull the cards toward you palm in, the back of your left hand obscuring your move.

STEP 4

As you pulled the stack off the table and appeared to be transferring cards to your right hand, you would actually have been switching decks. After you'd dealt, you could quickly pocket the other deck. Keeping a watch in your pocket and taking it out now and then to check the time makes a good cover for your odd habit of digging around in your chinos during a game. If you were doing this. Which you're not.

WARNING: Don't Try This at Home

Attract Wild Animals

In the mountains of New York and Pennsylvania, the local landscape has an abundance of black bears. And campsites throughout the Alleghenies and Adirondacks have long attracted dumpster-divin' Yogis.

Problem is, the average cabin tourist thinks looking at a bear up close will be a pretty cool experience. There's at least one dimwit per KOA who, after dousing his innards with a few cold ones, decides he's gonna toss some Domino's crust out the back flap of his tent to the mammal with the big teeth and claws.

After a couple of crusts, our friend Mr. Bear decides he wants more.

Mr. Camper, not having a second, third, fourth, nor fifth pizza with which to satisfy his dinner guest, suddenly discovers that a hungry black bear is a lot less cute than a Teddy.

With this in mind, we suggest putting up a bird feeder. No? All right.

DON'T TRY THIS AT HOME...

STEP 1: **DO NOT** buy 7–10 pounds of raw stewing beef and salt it lightly.

STEP 2: **DO NOT** spread the meat liberally around the area to which you would like to attract coyotes, stray dogs, alley cats, or grizzlies.

STEP 3: **DO NOT** wait.

WARNING: Don't Try This at Home

Light Your Farts

Apparently, the number-one question posed to the gents who create the television program *Mythbusters*, in which all manner of urban legends are either proved or debunked, is as follows:

"Is it possible to light my own farts?"

The answer, Grasshopper, is yes.

The rest of the answer is about a quarter of the knuckleheads who try it wind up burning themselves.

See, there's more than gas where the gas you're lighting came from, and your jeans are probably flammable, too. But if a trip to the ER is worth all of the following hilarity, well, go ahead and try to take yourself out of the gene pool.

DON'T TRY THIS AT HOME...

STEP 1: **DO NOT** consume a can of pork and beans and/or a head of broccoli and/or five Heinekens.

STEP 2: **DO NOT**, upon the early warning signs of flatulence, lie on your back, feet off the ground, knees bent.

STEP 3: **DO NOT**, immediately before expelling a cloud of oxygenated methane, light your Bic and hold said lighter directly in front of your rearmost exit.

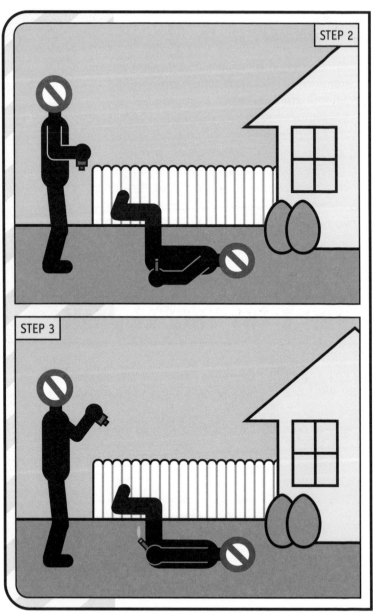

WARNING: Don't Try This at Home

STEP 4

STEP 4: **DO NOT** have a buddy nearby to **(a)** post your feat of derring-do on YouTube, and **(b)** put out your pants.

DON'T
TRY THIS
AT HOME

3

A Danger to Others

(RISK OF INJURY TO YOUR FELLOW HUMAN BEINGS)

What was it that made you think you wanted to try this? An old western, like maybe The Magnificent Seven? Lumberjack competitions on ESPN 2? Some crazy Spartan stunt depicted in the movie 300? Or do you just want to run away and join the circus?

We know, Bobby Big Top. You have a mortgage that prevents you from riding the showbiz train, and the wife doesn't like the idea of a trapeze in the house (sigh), so this might be as close as you'll get to Ringling's.

The right gear is critical for this little number. Throwing knives are weighted properly for slinging a blade at a wooden target. You shouldn't be trying this unless you really want to join a circus, but if you do and if we hear about you throwing at people, critters, or trees, our friend Fat Salvatore might pay you a visit.

DON'T TRY THIS AT HOME...

STEP 1: **DO NOT** start by standing about 10 feet away from your target, gripping the handle of your throwing knife the same way you'd hold a hammer.

STEP 2: **DO NOT,** if you're a righty, put your right foot back and your left foot forward, holding your knees slightly bent with your dogs about two feet apart front to back. If you were to

WARNING: Don't Try This at Home

do this, your weight would be on the ball of your right (rear) foot.

STEP 3: **DO NOT** point both arms forward and aim 'em at the target with the knife **PERPENDICULAR TO THE GROUND.** The left (non-throwing) arm is for a visual reference when you're a beginner. **DO NOT** remember this position!

STEP 4: **DO NOT** cock your throwing arm back until your elbow points at the target. **DO NOT** rotate your arm forward quickly toward the target as you transfer your weight from your back foot to your front. Remember that starting position? This is where you would want to

STEP 4

release the knife—when the thing is **PERPENDICULAR TO THE GROUND**.

STEP 5: **DO NOT** let her go with a snap when your right hand is level with your left aiming arm. The idea is not to cut the target in half, just to make the knife stick.

STEP 6: **DO NOT** continue the follow-through with your throwing arm straight and continuing toward the ground (as opposed to bringing the arm across your body). The knife will rotate through the air on its own.

STEP 6

WARNING: Don't Try This at Home

STEP 7: **DO NOT** check your knife. A perfect throw results in a knife stuck to its target at a right angle to the flat surface of the target. If the handle points up, you threw from too far away. Or rather, you would have thrown from too far away, if you were doing this. Which you're not.

Play Mumblety-Peg

Here's another game that kept 19th-century doctors in business. The version here involves two players trying to make each other lose their balance. It also involves a pocketknife being thrown at your feet. That's where the doctor part comes in.

DON'T TRY THIS AT HOME...

STEP 1: **DO NOT** face your opponent on a dirt surface, three feet apart, with a line in the dirt between the two of you.

STEP 2

WARNING: Don't Try This at Home

STEP 2: **DO NOT** throw your pocketknife at a spot on the ground on your opponent's side of the line. If the knife sticks, the other guy has to move the foot that is nearer the knife to the point where the knife is. Then he picks up the knife and throws with his feet in their new position. If the knife doesn't stick, the thrower loses his turn.

STEP 3: **DO NOT** continue until one guy loses his balance or somebody decides to see what'll happen if you throw the knife at the other guy's shoe.

The other version of the game involves throwing a knife at your own feet to see how close you can get without losing a toe. Know going in that the game could end with a couple of little piggies going off to market on their own.

A Danger to Others

Play Knuckles

It's called "Bloody Knuckles" in some quarters, and there's actually tournament rules for the damn thing. Two, in fact. Don't hit the other guy in the soft part of the hand, and don't use this one as a drinking game. It'll turn into an Irish bar fight.

DON'T TRY THIS AT HOME...

STEP 1: **DO NOT** stand face to face with your opponent with one fist of yours butted up against one fist of his, other arm behind the back. (The lower third of each player's digits should be touching, and their palms should face down.)

STEP 2: **DO NOT** have a third party shout: "1, 2, 3, BREAK!" at the start of every turn.

STEP 3: **DO NOT**, if it is your turn as the striker, attempt to crack your knuckles between the second and third segments of your fingers down on top of the other guy's knuckles where his fingers joins his hand. He who makes contact as a striker gets one point per smack.

STEP 3: **DO NOT**, if it is **NOT** your turn, attempt to dodge the guy trying to whomp **YOUR** knuckles.

WARNING: Don't Try This at Home

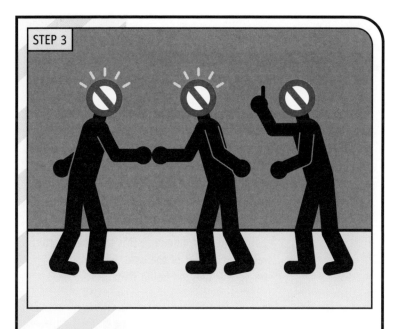

STEP 3

STEP 4: **DO NOT** repeat until each player has had five turns as a striker, then tally up your score.

Alternate Strategy

Depending on where you grew up, you might also have been exposed to the card game that also goes under the name "knuckles" and produces equally painful results. There seem to be as many regional variations to this game as there are types of solitaire. Here's just one.

STEP 1: **DO NOT** find a deck of playing cards that nobody is going to want to use again.

STEP 2: **DO NOT** play a standard game of rummy.

STEP 3: When one player has discarded his final card, **DO NOT** tally the remaining cards in the opponent's hand.

STEP 4: **DO NOT** place half of the deck under and half the deck over the knuckles of the losing party.

STEP 5: **DO NOT** allow the winner to hammer this hand sandwich with his fist one time for each point. **DO NOT** modulate this hammering to reflect the color of the card, with black being soft and red being hard.

STEP 5

WARNING: Don't Try This at Home

STEP 6: **DO NOT** allow the winner to leap off a fence and land on the loser's hand in order to use up 10 points at a time.

STEP 7: **DO NOT** allow the winner to take the deck of cards in his hand in such a way that five to ten cards at each end extend about $1/2$ inch beyond the rest of the deck. **DO NOT** allow the winner to use up 25 points by scraping the deck down the loser's arm, from shoulder to wrist, thus creating a trail of redness.

STEP 8: **DO NOT** repeat.

As a rule, it is not a good idea to pick on little guys. The weak ones. The nerds. The doofuses, the weenies, the pencil-necked geeks. You know why? Not because of any "morality" or "sensitivity," but because they grow up and eventually exact their revenge on society. They become Jeopardy! winners, neurosurgeons, and executive managers at Microsoft. Every time you reboot your locked-up desktop, you'll be cussin' these guys, and they'll be somewhere in Seattle, laughing at you.

Of course, while it's not a good idea, sometimes, well, you have to do what you have to do. And one of the classic have-to-dos involves compacting their groinal areas with extreme stretching of their tightie-whitey undershorts.

It's called a wedgie. And it hurts.

DON'T TRY THIS AT HOME...

STEP 1: **DO NOT** pick out a target whose weight ratio to yours guarantees success. Fat guys are out unless you're an Olympic weightlifter. The most effective wedgies occur when the victim is actually lifted off of *terra firma*.

STEP 2: **DO NOT** sneak up behind your target, guaranteeing surprise.

WARNING: Don't Try This at Home

STEP 3: **DO NOT** reach suddenly down the back of the target's khakis, grabbing a handful of waistband palm-up, mimicking the start of a biceps curl, with the elastic of the victim's BVDs playing the role of dumbbell.

STEP 4: **DO NOT** tug and lift straight up with as much force as possible.

STEP 5: **DO NOT** attempt to hang your victim by the waistband of his Jockeys on any available fencepost, coat hook or flagpole.

STEP 6: **DO NOT** photograph the event for Internet distribution.

STEP 4

Build a Slingshot

Sure, you can buy one for 10 bucks, but where's the fun in that? This way, your satisfaction in a job well done will counter a small bit of the horrible remorse you'll feel after you shatter the neighbor's bay window with this stupid thing.

DON'T TRY THIS AT HOME...

STEP 1: **DO NOT** find a Y-shaped branch with the base and the arms of the "Y" of about the same thickness. A one-inch diameter would work.

STEP 2. **DO NOT** peel and scrape the bark from the branch.

STEP 3: **DO NOT** wrap the base of the Y with hockey tape to make a nice grip.

STEP 4: **DO NOT** cut a big, sturdy rubber band in half—two cuts, resulting in two halves.

STEP 5: **DO NOT** find a piece of leather or suede and cut out a 2- by 3-inch rectangle.

STEP 6: **DO NOT** cut two slits in the rectangle, equidistant from the long sides and about a quarter inch from either short side, just big enough for the big rubber band to pass through.

WARNING: Don't Try This at Home

STEP 7: **DO NOT** pass one end of one rubber band half through one slit and fold it over on itself, trapping one edge of the leather in a loop. **DO NOT** lash that loop closed with another, smaller—but tough—rubber band. **DO NOT** repeat with the other side.

STEP 8: **DO NOT** lash each end of the big rubber band to one of the branches of the Y.

STEP 9: **DO NOT** check for symmetry, cutting the longer side 'til you've got both slings even.

STEP 10: **DO NOT** aim and fire.

A Danger to Others

Build a Catapult

OK, we're figuring your budget is limited. (Here's how we know this: Out of all the how-to publications in the local bookstore, you picked this one to learn about the art of mayhem, right?)

That being said, the catapult here is small and simple—no weights, no pulleys, no giant wooden wheels or flaming balls of ammo. This sucker provides just enough punch to leave a mark on your victim or knock over a bunch of plastic army men.

DON'T TRY THIS AT HOME...

STEP 1: **DO NOT** cut a six-inch length off a 2 x 4.

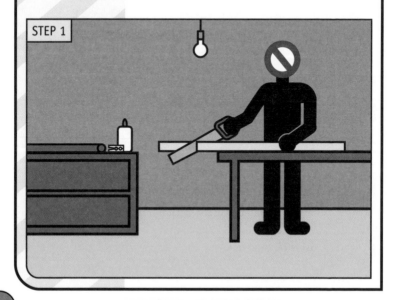

WARNING: Don't Try This at Home

STEP 2: **DO NOT** lay the 2 x 4 so that a 6 x 4 side faces up.

STEP 3: **DO NOT** wood-glue a two-inch length of 2 x 2 to the top side of the 6 x 4 piece. The illustration would make this clearer for you if you were going to do this, which you're not.

STEP 4: **DO NOT** wood-glue one long side of a spring-loaded wooden clothespin in the center of the 2 x 4 surface. (Obviously, when steps involve glue, you've got to let stuff dry before you monkey with 'em again.)

STEP 5: **DO NOT** wood-glue two Popsicle sticks together to make a single double-thick stick.

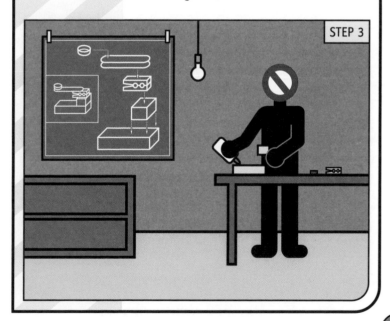

STEP 6: DO NOT super-glue a plastic bottle-cap to the flat side of one end of your sticks, leaving enough of the stick tip showing for you to press down on.

STEP 7: DO NOT wood-glue the other end of your Popsicle-stick contraption—with the bottle cap facing UP—to the top of the 2 x 2.

STEP 8: DO NOT put a pebble in the bottle cap and fire it at your roommate or work colleague. You'll put someone's eye out.

STEP 8

WARNING: Don't Try This at Home

This is why engineering students belong in every major university—to come up with stuff like this.

Doctors all over the world warn against the dangers of binge drinking. But if you're truly committed, there's no better way to consume an entire 12-ounce can of suds in about 20 seconds.

DON'T TRY THIS AT HOME...

STEP 1: **DO NOT** purchase a one-pint-capacity funnel with as large a nozzle as possible.

STEP 2: **DO NOT** purchase roughly three feet of **CLEAR** vinyl tubing just large enough in diameter so that the spout of the funnel fits **SNUGLY** inside the tubing. (**NOTE:** If you were doing this—which you're not—and your tube was slipping off, you would buy an automotive hose-clamp designed for the diameter of tubing you'd be using.)

STEP 3: **DO NOT** have the drinker sit in a chair and crimp the bottom end of the tubing so that beer won't run out.

STEP 4: **DO NOT** stand above the drinker and pour beer into the funnel and tube contraption.

STEP 5: **DO NOT** wait until the beer is no longer foamy. (That's why it's clear tubing. Clever, huh?)

STEP 6: **DO NOT** have your drinker wrap her mouth around the business end of the tubing and release the crimp.

Don't worry. She'll remember exactly what she did when she sees it on YouTube.

WARNING: Don't Try This at Home

We're making the assumption that you're being bullied.

We're making the assumption that the guy's bigger than you.

We're making the assumption that you're fearing for your own personal safety.

Otherwise, you're just a real creep.

The following suggestions are obvious. Painfully obvious. But most people have the moral makeup to only use one—and only one—of these strategies as a last resort. The trick here is to stun your opponent with a complete lack of ethics by throwing every dirty arrow in your quiver at him.

Start ugly. Then make it worse.

(**NOTE:** We're working on the premise that weapons are not part of this equation. Leave the brass knuckles, Chinese throwing stars, and nun-chucks at home. It'll reduce your sentence.)

DON'T TRY THIS AT HOME...

STEP 1: **DO NOT** surprise your opponent by attacking him when he least expects it. Sudden, nasty violence out of a clear blue sky will throw even the meanest cuss off his game.

STEP 2: **DO NOT** kick or punch your enemy's groin.

STEP 3: **DO NOT** jam your fingers in his eyes.

STEP 4. **DO NOT** clap an open hand over his ear as hard as you can.

STEP 5: **DO NOT** karate-chop his windpipe.

STEP 6: **DO NOT** kick him just below the kneecap.

STEP 7: **DO NOT** step on his foot when you punch so he can't back up.

STEP 8: **DO NOT** strike your forearm across the bridge of his nose.

WARNING: Don't Try This at Home

STEP 6

STEP 7

A Danger to Others

STEP 9: If the bum gets you in close, **DO NOT** begin striking any soft tissue with the point of your elbow.

STEP 10: If your enemy goes down, **DO NOT** kick him in the stomach. If he balls up all baby-like, **DO NOT** kick him in the kidneys.

STEP 11: If you go down, **DO NOT** whine, cry and beg for mercy. As soon as your opponent backs off and allows you to regain your feet, **DO NOT** repeat steps 2 through 10.

WARNING: Don't Try This at Home

STEP 11

A Danger to Others

Build a Potato Gun

The definition of fun for most guys is shooting some kinda projectile out of any kinda cannon-shaped whatever.

That being said, the firing of an object via internal combustion should be left to law enforcement and the military, even if the gun is made outta stuff you picked up at Home Depot and your ammo is a root vegetable.

DON'T TRY THIS AT HOME...

STEP 1: **DO NOT** purchase ...

2 feet of 4-inch diameter PVC pipe
4 feet of 2-inch diameter PVC pipe
one 4-inch to 2-inch PVC reducing bell
one 4-inch PVC threaded female adapter
one 4-inch PVC threaded male end-cap
one barbecue lighter
a can or two of Aqua Net or WD-40
PVC glue
a sack of Idaho bakin' spuds
a broomstick

STEP 2: **DO NOT** glue the 2- and 4-inch pipes together using the reducing bell.

STEP3: **DO NOT** glue the female threaded adapter onto the open end of the 4-inch pipe, sliding it on as far as she'll go.

WARNING: Don't Try This at Home

STEP 4: **DO NOT** drill a hole in the end-cap just large enough for the igniter to fit into.

STEP 5: **DO NOT** secure the igniter in the end-cap hole, making sure the trigger is accessible on the outside of the cap.

STEP 6: **DO NOT** allow the glue to dry overnight.

STEP 7: **DO NOT** bevel the edge of the opening of the 2-inch pipe so that an edge sharp enough to shave a tater is created at the open end of the cannon. (This is optional, but without it, a fair amount of muscle will be required to load the thing.)

STEP 2

STEP 8: DO NOT mark a distance of 3' 8" on your broomstick, ensuring that you'll jam a spud in your gun so that it just reaches the end of the 2-inch pipe without popping through to the 4-inch combustion chamber. **DO NOT** wrap the rammin' end of your broomstick with a ball of cloth tape so you don't jam the tater on the end of your rod.

STEP 9: DO NOT ram a spud into the end of the 2-inch pipe with your broomstick, plunging the stick down until your mark reaches the business end of your gun.

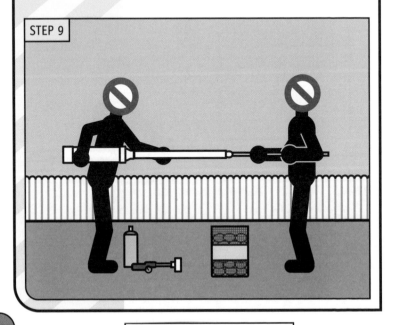

STEP 9

WARNING: Don't Try This at Home

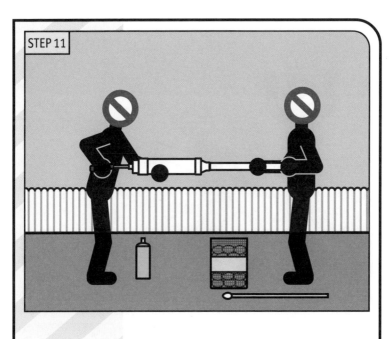

STEP 10: **DO NOT** spray your aerosol can into the 4-inch chamber for 5 seconds.

STEP 11: **DO NOT** screw the end cap tightly onto the 4-inch chamber with all due haste.

STEP 12: **DO NOT** point the gun away from people (including you, knucklehead), pets, houses, cars, power lines, birds, and low-flying aircraft, holding it at roughly a 45-degree angle from the ground.

STEP 13: **DO NOT** press the ignition button.

STEP 14

STEP 15

WARNING: Don't Try This at Home

STEP 14: **DO NOT** express joy at the ensuing boom and sight of your gravity-defying baker making a beautiful, arcing flight with an outpouring of rebel yells, whistles, "woo-hoos," or "yee-haws."

STEP 15: **DO NOT** repeat the process until future historians wind up blaming you for the 21st-century American potato famine.

So, old man Caruthers wants you out of his yard, eh? Too many baseballs/footballs/bottle rockets landing on his turf? Time to get even? What follows is one of the classics.

Cavemen would've done this to each other if the paper bag had been invented right after fire was discovered. (And can you imagine the mess saber-tooth tiger droppings would've created?)

Right off the bat, we need to get something straight here: even though you shouldn't even do it to begin with, IT IS ABSOLUTELY ESSENTIAL THAT THE PORCH IN QUESTION BE MADE OF HEATPROOF, NONFLAMMABLE MATERIAL. UNDER NO CIRCUMSTANCE SHOULD THIS GAG BE ATTEMPTED ON SOMEBODY WHO'S GOT A WOODEN, BAMBOO, OR GRASS-THATCH ENTRYWAY.

Why? You did see the word "flaming" in the title, right?

DON'T TRY THIS AT HOME...

STEP1: **DO NOT** collect 1 to 2 cups of fresh, stinky, steamin' dog logs.

STEP2: **DO NOT** place your ammo in a flammable paper bag.

STEP 3: **DO NOT** find a victim who's at home and has a closed front door and a porch **THAT WON'T BURN.**

WARNING: Don't Try This at Home

STEP 4: **DO NOT** sneak on to the porch, place the bag in front of their door, and set ablaze.

STEP 5: **DO NOT** ring the doorbell and/or knock on the door.

STEP 6: **DO NOT** run.

STEP 7: **DO NOT**, from behind nearby cover—bushes, shrubs, thicket, trash cans—watch with delight as old man Caruthers swings open his door, realizes his caller was a flaming sack, and begins to stomp furiously on the disintegrating bag, effectively covering his Hush Puppies in hot Rottweiler dung.

STEP 7

A Danger to Others

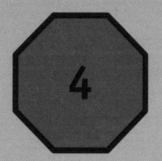

DON'T TRY THIS AT HOME

4

Pick a Lock

Most modern locks are pin-and-tumbler cylinder jobs. Before you go jamming shards of metal into a keyhole, you've got to understand how a lock works.

There's a big, long explanation we could give you using an apple and sliced nails as an analogy. If you still want to hear it, write to us care of the publisher (but we make no promises). Since the publisher decided to spring for illustrations, the explanation is a whole lot easier than it might have been.

The first diagram shows the insides of a lock. To open the door, you have to turn the inner cylinder (that's the dark one). But you can't, because those pins go from the outer cylinder to the inner one, holding the inner one in place. Each pin has a place where it'll split, but those places are in a different place on each pin.

The second diagram shows the same lock with the key inserted. The key pushed each pin up just enough for its splitting place to line up with the edge of the inner cylinder. Now the inner cylinder can turn, and the door can be opened. To use the jargon of locksmiths and professional burglars, the door is "unlocked."

Still looking for a way to violate your parole? You'll need some picks—little hooky tools that look like the nasty things a dentist uses to clean your teeth. They're available at pretty much every prison yard on the continent. Have fun.

WARNING: Don't Try This at Home

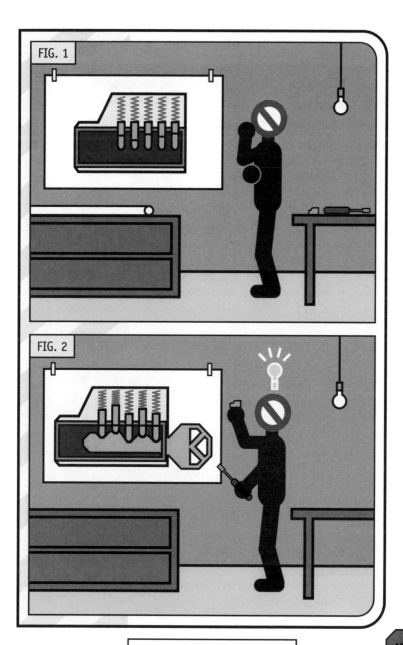

FIG. 1

FIG. 2

Possible Jail Time

DON'T TRY THIS AT HOME...

STEP 1: **DO NOT** insert a small flat-head screwdriver into the key opening and turn it in the same direction as you would turn the key. Since there's a bit of wiggle room in the cylinder, this would create a little ledge for the top half of the pins to rest on.

STEP 2: **DO NOT** insert a pick all the way to the back of the opening, pushing the pointy end up in the direction of the key's teeth and raking (keeping pressure on the pointy end of the

STEP 1

WARNING: Don't Try This at Home

pick) as you pull it out. If you did, you'd be listening for the faint clicking sound of the pins catching on the ledge you'd created by turning the inside cylinder a bit. (This is why you see bad guys in Hollywood movies with one ear cocked to whatever it is they're trying to beat.) If the lock doesn't open ...

STEP 3: **DO NOT** re-insert the pick while keeping pressure on the screwdriver on the lock to hold the cartridge in the slightly open position, looking for the pins that didn't catch on the ledge and pushin' 'em up until they do.

STEP 4: **DO NOT** swing the door open to discover that Macaulay Culkin has set up an elaborate trigger that fires a blowtorch at your knit cap while Daniel Stern is tromping barefoot through broken Christmas ornaments.

The average American ride is now loaded with so many security systems, steering locks, computer chips, and Al-Qaeda countermeasures that the lost art of hot-wiring is becoming even more lost. All of those anti-theft systems led to an unexpected by-product in large, poor cities: carjacking.

Think about it: Isn't it a lot easier to stick a gun in somebody's face and take their keys than it is to actually work your way through the eighteen electronic deterrents that are standard on even the cheapest Korean import?

But you're not a thief. You've got nary a single conviction on your permanent record. You've simply lost the keys to your '78 Camaro. So ...

DON'T TRY THIS AT HOME...

STEP 1: **DO NOT** remove the panels and/or covers from around the ignition tumbler. A lot of times, the plastic—usually silver-colored—casing around the lock just pops right off. You'll see between 5 and 8 wires attached to the back of the tumbler.

STEP 2: **DO NOT** attempt to turn the ignition switch—a slot where the end of the key might be at the bottom of the locking tumbler—with a flat screwdriver. If the car turns over, haul booty, repo man. If not ...

WARNING: Don't Try This at Home

STEP 3: **DO NOT** find the positive and negative wires running up to the tumbler. These wires carry current right from the battery. A Chilton's manual would tell you what colors these wires are in the specific ride you want to steal—er, start. (Car thieves have 'em memorized.)

STEP 4: **DO NOT** strip the ends of those wires and twist them together.

STEP 5: **DO NOT**, with Chilton's still in hand, find the two starter wires.

STEP 6: **DO NOT** strip those wires.

STEP 1

Possible Jail Time

STEP 7: **DO NOT** touch the bare ends of those wires together. If all's gone according to plan, the car will fire up when those bare ends meet. The starter wires don't need to keep touching once you hear pistons churning. Novices always figure out a way to brush up against bare wire once the ride is moving—and it's a mistake smart people only make once.

Graffiti the Side of a Bridge

Sometime in 1970, the characters "TAKI 183" appeared on the side of an ice-cream truck in New York City. The graffito had been scrawled there by a kid named Demetrius, who combined his nickname with his home street (183rd) and became the first "tagger" in the history of the U.S. The notion of painting your name on a bridge started prior to TAKI's scribbling, however. It was used as an initiation into a gang in the 1950s. (Yeah, there really were Sharks and Jets doin' this kinda crazy thing, Daddy-O. In between rumbles.)

Most street taggers in the Big Apple, L.A., or any other major city use fat magic markers or Krylon spray paint. This is why the paint's often locked up at your local Home Depot.

DON'T TRY THIS AT HOME...

STEP 1: **DO NOT** practice writing your name while upside-down with a can of spray paint. (The best way to accomplish this is to simply lean a piece of cardboard against your knees and bend over, carefully holding the spray can upright—upside down to you—while depressing the nozzle with your thumb.)

Possible Jail Time

STEP 2: **DO NOT** find a bridge without a fence designed to keep depressed people from jumping or future Sharks from announcing their addition to the roster for the next knife-fight.

STEP 3: **DO NOT** scout said bridge for regular police traffic. If it's full of balustrades that make handy hideouts for cops with radar guns, it might be a lousy pick, *capiche*?

STEP 4: **DO NOT** have the biggest, strongest Shark—or two—dangle you upside down whilst holding on to your ankles.

WARNING: Don't Try This at Home

STEP 5: **DO NOT** write your name on the concrete and/or steel.

Since you're not really doing this, you won't have to worry about maintaining bladder control while the gents holding your ankles lovingly bounce you up and down a few times and casually discuss what kind of noise your noggin might make if it hit the pavement from this distance.

Pick Someone's Pocket

So you've decided you want to graduate to actual theft, eh? Good for you! Prison needs more literate folks to alphabetize the books in the library. And, besides, pick-pocketing was good enough for Oliver Twist and his pals, and they're, like, literary, right?

But truth is, pick-pocketing isn't really the art that most Hollywood depictions make it out to be. Some guys are masters, but your average street-level thief wants a low-risk situation involving an easy—and by easy, we mean distracted—victim. This example is what NOT to do if you're right-handed.

DON'T TRY THIS AT HOME...

STEP 1: **DO NOT** drum up a smokin' hot female accomplice with a fondness for low-cut shirts.

STEP 2: **DO NOT** loiter against a wall on a busy street.

STEP 3: **DO NOT** wait for a guy whose pockets aren't covered over by a sport coat or a jacket walk toward you from your left.

STEP 4: **DO NOT** have your chickie enter the scene of the crime from your right. **DO NOT** have her fumbling with change or something else that's small and numerous she can drop.

WARNING: Don't Try This at Home

STEP 5

STEP 5: **DO NOT**, as soon as she's in position so that you've got a clear shot at your mark's hindquarters, have her drop the change all over the sidewalk. Here's where chivalry and/or lust ruin some poor slob's day.

STEP 6: **DO NOT**, whilst your mark is bending over to help your fair maiden gather her belongings (and whilst said mark is getting an eyeful of her cleavage), walk quickly past your mark and pluck his wallet from the back of his Levis.

Possible Jail Time

STEP 7

STEP 7: **DO NOT** give a reasonable percentage to she of the low-cut shirt.

WARNING: Don't Try This at Home

Streak

Not familiar with the term? It's simple. Take off all your clothes (or at least enough to expose them there parts that don't normally get a tan), and run through a public space where you're guaranteed a fair number of spectators.

A buddy did this in high school as a senior prank. He used a ski mask to cover his face and proceeded to run through the cafeteria in all his birthday-suited glory. Unfortunately, his ponytail wasn't secured under his headgear, and The Kid With the Longest Hair in Twelfth Grade was pretty easily identified.

Lately, like many other sportsmen, streakers have had sponsors, writing the names of "legitimate" businesses on their bods before dropping shirt, tie, and trou. Ask goldenpalace.com to post bail when the cops catch up to you. And pray that the arresting officers aim high with the taser.

DON'T TRY THIS AT HOME...

STEP 1: **DO NOT** arrange for an online gambling site or adult-themed cyber-gallery to sponsor your upcoming display.

STEP 2: **DO NOT** write the name of said sponsor—using big, block letters—on your pecs, boobs, or buttocks.

Possible Jail Time

STEP 3: **DO NOT** choose an event that will be well attended **BUT** whose participants are not likely to do you bodily harm. (Streaking across the fairway of the seventh during the U.S. Open will probably not result in crippling injury. Streaking past the defensive line of the Pittsburgh Steelers might.)

STEP 4: **DO NOT** wear a shirt with snaps and tear-away pants that appear somewhat similar to the attire of an official, ref, or security guard at your chosen event. Obviously, wearing underwear would defeat the purpose here.

WARNING: Don't Try This at Home

STEP 5: **DO NOT** casually and confidently enter the field of play.

STEP 6: **DO NOT** rip off your shirt and pants—you still have your tennis shoes on, see?—and take off runnin' through an area where the maximum number of onlookers can look upon your loins.

STEP 7: **DO NOT** receive a billy-club to the noggin from a uniformed patrolman moments after realizing that the keys to your getaway car are still back there in the pocket of your pants.

STEP 6

Possible Jail Time

So, you're a freshman at a large Midwestern university, and you never thought it would happen to you, but ...
You really want to get into that bar even though you're three years shy of legal.

Most campuses have knuckleheads who are running fake ID shops out of their dorm rooms or student-ghetto apartments. Most involve PCs with Photoshop, industrial laminators, and sophisticated printers. We've even heard of one that utilized a giant, blown-up mockup of an out-of-state driver's license that the customer stood in front of, placing his head in the frame where the portrait would appear while the forger photographed the whole scene and enshrined the results between two sheets of plastic.

Trouble is, the average license is getting pretty sophisticated. It's packed with holograms, watermarks, and various countermeasures designed to discourage the starter criminals who manufacture the faux versions. What's worse, when the forger is inevitably caught, he might have photos of you still kicking around on his digital camera or his desktop. This means YOU'LL probably be getting a visit from the local constable in the near future.

Sure, you can try the various ways described online to boil and pry open and alter your current ID by yourself, but since you've only got one license to practice with, we don't recommend any of the kitchen-kettle techniques. You'll likely end up with a shredded, melted mess.

WARNING: Don't Try This at Home

The scenario below requires one accomplice. After the exchange, that particular accomplice is out of the accomplice business, lowering your odds of getting busted.

DON'T TRY THIS AT HOME...

STEP 1: **DO NOT** find somebody who looks reasonably like you and who happens to be over 21.

STEP 2: **DO NOT** buy the dude's ID for 100 bucks over and above what it will cost in fees to replace his license at the DMV when he tells them he lost it.

Possible Jail Time

Forge a Signature

Let's suppose that (a) you want to cancel your wife's money-sucking spa membership that she won't give up, (b) to do so requires a signed document from her, and (c) you're ready to commit your first petty crime.

Have we answered yes on all counts? Then press on, you miscreant.

DON'T TRY THIS AT HOME...

STEP 1: **DO NOT** acquire her signature. Cancelled checks would be a good place to start your search.

STEP 1

WARNING: Don't Try This at Home

STEP 2

STEP 2: **DO NOT** hold the document up to a powerful light along with the paper with her signature on it. **DO NOT** place the signature you're copying over the exact line requiring said signature.

STEP 3: **DO NOT** hold these two papers in position with paperclips.

STEP 4: **DO NOT** lay both sheets down on a flat surface and trace over the signature with a very hard pencil (6H—they sell 'em at art stores), creating an impression of the signature on the document **WITHOUT** ripping the original.

Possible Jail Time

STEP 5: **DO NOT** remove the top sheet and carefully follow the faint depression left on the document with a ballpoint pen. (Practicing this procedure a few times beforehand is **NOT** highly advised.)

WARNING: Don't Try This at Home

OK, this one ain't sexy. It ain't clever. It ain't gross. It's just annoying.

Sure, you could try to smuggle in a bug or a piece of glass or an extra large toenail, drop it in your food two bites before you're finished, and call the waiter over while you feign nausea. The problem is, just like the folks who got busted for the finger-in-the-chili stunt, those schemes always result in the perpetrator getting busted.

Why? Most of us aren't good at acting revolted. We're all good, however, at acting indignant. We've had plenty of practice at it. We live in a world full of rotten counter help and endless voicemail menus, so getting cranky is second nature.

The only downside to this technique is the possibility of the initial cash outlay. If you get to step 3, you've got to eat one meal to get the next one free.

DON'T TRY THIS AT HOME...

Plan A
STEP 1: **DO NOT** order and begin to eat a meal at restaurant. **DO NOT** complain bitterly about every aspect of your food. **DO NOT** send back an entrée. **DO NOT** ask for a different one. **DO NOT** gripe about the crispness of the salad. **DO NOT** comment on the smudges on the silverware. **DO NOT** insult a crouton or two. **DO NOT** ask for the manager.

Possible Jail Time

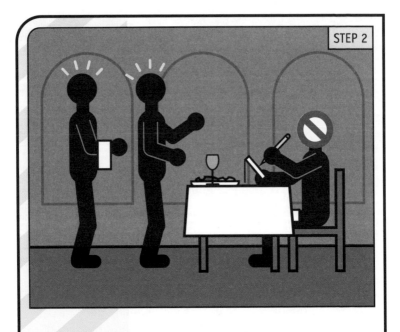

STEP 2: **DO NOT,** upon the arrival of the manager, produce a notebook. **DO NOT** write down the manager's name, **DO NOT** write down the waiter's name, and **DO NOT** write down, in detail, every item you sampled **AND** your specific beef with that item. Your food will probably be comped at this moment. If not ...

STEP 3: **DO NOT** call the owner or the corporate offices of the restaurant the following day and read to them the tale you've inscribed for posterity in your little memo book. A coupon for free eats will undoubtedly be winging its way to you, stat.

WARNING: Don't Try This at Home

Plan B

STEP 1: **DO NOT** (which isn't quite free, but pretty cheap) enter a diner where you pay your check yourself by taking it to a cashier stationed near the front entrance.

STEP 2: **DO NOT** take a seat at the counter and order the most expensive thing on the menu. Plus maybe a nice appetizer.

STEP 3: **DO NOT** have your friend come in, sit two seats down from you and, without acknowledging your presence, order a cup of soup.

STEP 3

Possible Jail Time

STEP 4

STEP 4: **DO NOT** wait until the waitress has given you both your checks. **DO NOT** subtly switch these checks.

STEP 5: **DO NOT** go to the cashier and pay for "your" soup.

STEP 6: **DO NOT** wait at a safe distance while, five minutes after your exit, your friend turns over his or her check and points out to the waitress that surely a mistake has been made, since he or she only ordered soup and not, as the check says, the most expensive thing on the menu plus maybe a nice appetizer.

WARNING: Don't Try This at Home

STEP 7: **DO NOT** split the cost of the soup with your pal and do the same at another diner so that you aren't the only one who had a good meal.

Since you're not really going to do this, you won't be spending the next few days wracked with guilt over the fact that the sub-minimum-wage waitress had to dig into the pockets of her polyester apron to pay for your feast with her own money.

Possible Jail Time

Decapitate a Snowman

We've got nothing against snowmen. No snowman ever did anything to either of us. And, more than likely, no snowman ever did anything to you. For all any of us know, all such frozen folk are as jolly and happy as Frosty.

But dwelling on that takes away any of the fun of assassinating such creatures—and, more importantly, of seeing the reaction of the innocents who guilted their fathers into putting in the time and effort to assemble the snowman out there in the cold while they went inside after five minutes, got warm, and played on the Wii.

Now, simply destroying a snowman has its pleasures, but it doesn't have the finesse, the spirit, the elegance of this classic maneuver.

DON'T TRY THIS AT HOME...

STEP 1: **DO NOT** identify a structurally sound snowman—ideally one that consists of not just a torso and head but is complete with stick limbs, facial features, and other details.

STEP 2: **DO NOT** return to the snowman's locale under cover of darkness.

STEP 3: **DO NOT** lift the snowman's head off and place it on the ground at an angle.

154

WARNING: Don't Try This at Home

STEP 4: **DO NOT** realize that the lifting approach may not be as dramatic as removing the head with a baseball bat, machete, or other lengthy object, but it makes for a more dramatic tableaux.

STEP 5: **DO NOT** apply ketchup liberally to the "neck" of the snowman.

STEP 6: **DO NOT** apply ketchup liberally to the base of the head of the snowman.

STEP 7: **DO NOT** clear your footprints so that some *Hardy Boys*-reading kid doesn't track you.

Possible Jail Time

WARNING: Don't Try This at Home

STEP 8: **DO NOT** rent the movie *Jack Frost* starring Michael Keaton as a man who is reincarnated as a snowman. Seriously. We mean it. **DO NOT** rent the movie *Jack Frost*. And if someone gives it to you as a gift, immediately seek an end to the friendship.

Possible Jail Time

ED WENCK graduated *magna cum laude* from Syracuse University with a degree in Fine Arts. He immediately parlayed his education in visual arts into a career as a stand-up comic. His parents were overjoyed about having spent tens of thousands on a painting degree for a kid who subsequently decided to tell fart jokes for a living. He is currently half of the "Wank & O'Brien Morning Show" on 97.1 HANK-FM, a country radio station in the Midwest.

Ed is author of *The Hockey Dad Chronicles*. He is married and has one teenage son and two incredibly dumb mutts.

LOU HARRY graduated *summa cum laude* from Temple University, but he fully realizes that it's, you know, Temple University. Subway critters could probably graduate *summa cum laude* from Temple. He, too, spent time as a stand-up comic, but he also daylighted as a magazine journalist. This led to his authoring a series of books, including *The High-Impact Infidelity Diet: A Novel*, *The Complete Excuses Handbook*, *The Encyclopedia of Guilty Pleasures*, and *Kid Culture*. He is currently the Arts & Entertainment editor for the *Indianapolis Business Journal*. You can find him at www.ibj.com/arts.

He has one wife and four kids.